AFTE

N. S. THOMPSON

NEW WALK EDITIONS
Nottingham & Leicester

Acknowledgements
Most of these poems have appeared in the following journals: *The Hudson Review* (USA), *New Poetry Quarterly*, *New Walk*, *The Reader*, *The Spectator*, *Stand*. An earlier version of 'Odysseus after the Sirens' appeared in *New Writing 5* (Vintage/Arts Council, 1995). My thanks to the editors concerned.

Published by New Walk Editions
c/o Nick Everett, Centre for New Writing,
University of Leicester, LE1 7RH
and
c/o Rory Waterman,
Nottingham Creative Writing Hub,
Department of English, Philosophy and Communication,
Nottingham Trent University, NG11 8NS

ISBN: 978-1-8381153-0-2

Printed by imprintdigital, Upton Pyne, Exeter.

CONTENTS

AFTER WAR

'The Firs', 'Hillcrest', 'Innisfree'

i.

An aerial view. A brochure maps it out
And full possession guaranteed
Within the year: time for the prefab plots to sprout
Before the moves and backyards turn to seed.

ii.

Look, engines pushing upwards, shovels plough
Until the hill is taken, then a kerb
Whitewashed, Colonial style, now caps the brow
Once held by rosebay willow herb.

iii.

From smoke-black stations, city veterans
Ascend and, armed with suitcases, meet packed
Possessions dropped by green removal vans
To walls new-plastered, pale and cracked.

iv.

But after decoration, ground is gained:
Slit trenches, dug in by skeletal frames,
Hold nothing but the memories retained
By varnished pokerwork to post the names.

NISSEN HUT, 1960

Once camouflaged, a riddle turning rust,
It came to pieces by the golf course, links
At one end, new estate the other, dust
Caked round the lunettes of its iron sphinx.

When boys beat living daylight down its flank,
Cleared frogs out from its feline mouth, then spied
On couples courting with the truth, its rank
Old skeleton left nothing more to hide.

MESSAIEN: *QUARTET FOR THE END OF TIME*

First performance: Stalag VIII-A,
Görlitz (now Zgorzelec, Poland),
15th January 1941

i.

Wind soughs; rain soaks the ill-constructed camp
Whose wooden stamp
Is rigid with the staves and barbs of wire
On which his semi-quavers dance.

ii.

It is the end of time. The fall of France.
Could notes enhance
Men captured for an audience? Why are
Heads shaking, unbelieving, in the cold and damp?

SPEECHLESS

Austria was framed inside the dark brown prints
    Along the walls where glass reflections shone
Some light on them from cabinets with glints
    Of Meissen, Royal Vienna, crystal, bone

China, but tea was far more simple round
    A table spread with pickles, mayonnaise
And celery, then suddenly the sound
    Of chimes and we were shuffled to the chaise

Longue, ritual now broken like a spell,
    The concert broadcast on the radio
Significant – as far as we could tell –
    So sat in silence as it played to show

We had respect; our parents speechless, out
    Of depth, put on a brave front in the face
Of it… a piano trio was no doubt
    Embarrassing. If we felt out of place,

Miss Moore looked to the grand piano bought
    From what was left of Miss Sachs' family's wealth,
The stool raised to full height on which she taught
    Until rheumatics and her failing health

Stopped that. Then Miss Moore, jovial, benign,
    Flushed even deeper red to see Miss Sachs,
Her flatmate sunk in shawls, a silver line
    Of tears drawn down a face as pale as wax.

THE AGE OF RECONSTRUCTION

Blue sky betrays no telltale plume
Of smoke, a book of matches makes the rite
As small boys gather making room
Below the scaffold of a building site

For stolen spuds popped into ash.
The leader grins and grasps his grubby knees,
Then speaks out, grimly. Bold and brash
Words feed the flames. "You know what Japanese

Did during war?" His rival looks intense:
"That's nothing to what concentration camps
Would do!" Barbed wire coils off a fence
And hits a row of huts. A sandal stamps.

Boys circle, watching as the blows
And wrestling bodies exercise the will
Until the blackened twigs expose
The half-baked skins and appetite is still.

Above, it seems the daylight moon
Sits pale with conflict on its pockmarked face,
And nothing but a child's cartoon
For all it has to tell the human race.

A CITY GENTLEMAN (BROWSING THE OUTSIDE STOCK OF FOYLE'S)

Spines stiffen on a line of books
    Grained with thick dust, bleached by the sun,
Shoring a bookstore frontage up, Charing Cross Road,
        Mid-1950s:
A City Gent out, armed with brolly and a bowler, looks
    Along them one by one,
Eyes smartly weighing up this load
    Of square bashed stock as if

It formed a regiment,
    Clothbound and uniform,
For his inspection (some with wartime tags
        Still) in an awkward squad of learning on parade,
Half standing to attention, others slouched, backs bent
    From too much study. But they form
A line worth fighting for; the gentleman recalls sandbags
    Round walls for shock air-raid

Attacks along this curving street
    Where bombs fell in
And tried to blast a hole inside the city's heart.
        But walls withstood those ordered acts,
Books left like buildings, grey or shabby, but complete,
    Like him in pin-
Stripe suit, umbrella, bowler hat and part
    To play. Now, are these all the facts?

Along the street, the headlines lead
    With one word *Suez*… Here books catch his eye,
He wonders what, perhaps, his servants read,
        But then would never pry;
And as the thought of history fleetingly returns
    To him, he thumbs an old Theocritus,
Smiling a little sadly and then turns
    To take the Tube or catch a bus.

...WITH STRINGS

Black bow ties, violin case at their sides,
    Lou Kieveman, Victor Slatkin, Felix Katz,
        Wait for a streetcar in the sunshine, hats
    A gaudy pork pie, never kosher. Rides

In public pleasurable, out they go
    To play the concert hall. "You ever heard
        This new *meschugge* sax they call the 'Bird'?"
    "Ach, jazz with strings… Whatever would you know?"

Anomalous in hired tuxedo suits
    Beneath the snazzy hatbands of the year,
        They smile wry smiles - eyes nervous - but no fear
    (No way that they could be caught dead in zoots).

Across the summer of a New York spring
    They blink at music from a cellar. Rails
        Start rumbling, bringing back the camp details
    That hauled away small parcels tight with string.

Like children, shy, bemused by cattle trucks,
    They mount the steps in order to a seat,
        The cents still alien as they find their feet
    Amid the lurching and the sideways looks.

UBI SOLITUDINEM…

i.

Where lines of sightless brick create no bond,
Blind alleys mark a temporary state;
No future anywhere, no view beyond
Adobe architecture braced with tin:
The dry encampment's walls proliferate
And see how much confusion lies within:
No one could ever hope to find a home
Here in this endless repetition. No
One harbours any hope, albeit some
Dream of a settlement, when they can go…

ii.

Between his teeth, a small boy pulls the string
That drags his toy tank over shifting sands
Beyond the walls: the only solid thing
After the mine that blew away both hands.

A FIGURE ON THE BEACH

Cape Henry Light, Virginia

A dead beach after D-Day? Wave on wave
Pulled back sits innocent offshore,
Treading water in soft retreat. What can we save
Here? Sand, a pockmarked landscape, like the moon
Gleams bubble-clean, but drowned mementos score
The flats rising to dune

Left black with empty shells. No life is left.
The carcass of a horseshoe crab
Lies, helmet cleaned out, gritty in a sandy cleft,
The rest of its platoon washed on the wrack
While ocean, lurking for another stab
At them, waits to attack.

If only death were clean like this, you think,
Feet printing on the silk sea-sheen
Of sand: toes surface whiter than a clam, then sink
Below its gelid crystals, while you fish
An ocean of your thoughts for things to mean
Far more than what you wish.

As water sluices in a forceful motion
Down runnels of retreating tide,
Atlantic's breakers prance, white-plumed; the salt of ocean
Blown in your face; a noble glint of war
Beside the washed-up bodies left to ride
Is simply metaphor.

But in that confluence of sea and sky
And lump flesh landed on the beach
- Crabs, turtle turned land-mine, men o' war - you see fly
Along those sharply cresting waves a troop
Of coasting pelicans that drops from reach.
As if cut off, they stoop

And dip along a slow trough in the waves,
Absorbed perhaps, not drowned, then soar
Beyond the cutting crests. Knowing how each behaves,
They keep a figure. Man, the sad maroon,
Can only marvel from a sandy floor
On flats rising to dune.

A DIZZY ATMOSPHERE

Tombolo pineta, 1945

Entrenching tools hang idle. In the shade
New platforms bear the message now that Count
And Duke vacate the stage, a shanty town's
    Black markets where it's really made.

Am-lira rich deserters wait for whores
Bussed from Livorno, hip to stars with horns
Fresh from Big Apple; jelly-roll and pork
    Shake pup-tents, pines and PX stores.

Europa nurses Minos in the squeeze
For tins and Hershey bars. To get things straight
Girls struggle into nylons, left to face
    New standards swinging through the trees.

ODYSSEUS AFTER THE SIRENS

i.

Left standing in the Wakes, he knew the world
    Of loneliness when trudging ankle deep
Across deserted sand to building sites,
    Hoping to find a lost patrol or tank
Displaced among a line of oil drums
    Now lost in action, too, or buried in
A concrete culvert, trench or drift of sand.
    Undaunted, he hopped on his silver wheels,
An epic cycle launched in roaring trades
    En route towards adjacent districts where
The shops still opened selling model troops.

ii.

Stopped by a traffic island where a red
    Eye gleamed, he saw a zebra crossing, then
A beacon flashed on amber cellophane
    Across a window, drawn to shield its ranks
From mid-day sun; but half-day closing meant
    The shop was shut. Still dauntless, on he forged
To waves of traffic on a girder bridge,
    And heard the city sirens calling as
He swirled into the depths of streets, lost on
    A strand below bleak warehouse cliffs and came
To grief upon a bombsite left in weeds.

POLSKA KIEŁBASA

1950s

A Polish deli, Bury's covered market, town
    Of crumbling cotton, terraces shored up:
Men settled here as mill hands after war deprived
    Them of a home, when life turned upside down,
        Forced labour in the factories of Krupp
Miraculously survived…
    Now down a class or two, they let eyes feed as cuts
        Hit greaseproof paper, slices burst
With memories of the starving wooden huts
    As plain blue overalls stand in line and wait,
        But patiently relieved to state
    Polska kiełbasa not *Polnische wurst.*

Notes

'…With Strings': Charlie 'Bird' Parker first played with strings in Carnegie Hall in 1947, later at further concerts and studio recordings.

'*Ubi Solitudinem…*': the phrase is from Tacitus's *Agricola* where a Caledonian chieftain described Roman conquest as *ubi solitudinem faciunt, pacem appellant* (where they make a desert, they call it peace).

'A Dizzy Atmosphere': title of the be-bop standard recorded by Dizzy Gillespie and Charlie Parker in February 1945. Tombolo pine forest was a clandestine army deserters' camp near Pisa that became a notorious black market zone. *Am-lira* (Allied Military lira) were issued by the American forces in Italy from 1943-45.

'Odysseus After the Sirens': 'wakes' were once the traditional holidays in northern textile towns when the mills and many retailers closed for a week or two.